YOUR MARKETING ROAD MAP

5 Steps to Stop Overwhelm, Drive More Customers, and Accelerate Sales

LIZ PAPAGNI

Published by Liz Papagni
Copyright © 2020 by Liz Papagni
The unauthorized reproduction or distribution of this copyrighted work is illegal. Criminal copyright infringement, including infringement without monetary gain, is investigated by the Federal Bureau of Investigation and is punishable by up to 5 (five) years in federal prison and a fine of $250,000. No part of this book may be reproduced or transmitted in any form or by any means, electronic or mechanical, including photocopying, recording, or by any information storage and retrieval system, without permission in writing from the publisher, except in the case of brief quotations embodied in critical articles or reviews.
All rights reserved.
Graphic designer: Marla Shaw, Marla Shaw Graphic Design
Editor: Jennifer M. Barry
ISBN: 9798576105335

Contents

Acknowledgments	v
Preface	vii
Chapter 1	1
Chapter 2	15
Chapter 3	27
Chapter 4	35
Chapter 5	49
About the Author	71
One Last Thing	73
Appendix	75

Acknowledgments

My husband and two awesome boys for their love and support, and making my life complete.

My team for their continued dedication, commitment, and fabulousness.

My mastermind group for their encouragement, guidance, and friendship.

And my awesome clients for entrusting me to help them to build, grow, and expand their businesses.

Preface

HARNESSING THE POWER OF MARKETING

Oh, marketing: a word that has so much promise. When implemented correctly, marketing brings so much value to companies and organizations. It has the power to help them elevate their company, their brand, and revenues. But to many, marketing is about overwhelm, and confusion, and "How do I really use it to grow my business?"

The term "marketing" is perceived as broad to many, with most having varying definitions, thoughts, and preconceived ideas of what it means and delivers.

Sometimes the term marketing is used interchangeably with the term advertising, which is partially correct, but advertising doesn't come close to covering the full spectrum of benefits that marketing provides.

So what is marketing?

How is it really defined? Well, a recent definition from the American Marketing Association outlined it as "The activity, set of institutions, and processes for creating, communicating, delivering, and exchanging offerings that have value for customers, clients, partners, and society at large."

Does that make it clearer?

Probably not.

Marketing involves so much more than could be included in a one-sentence definition. When individuals or potential clients ask me what I do, I say, "I run a marketing and branding firm that works with established small and medium size business to help them rise above the competition, get more customers, and increase their revenue on a daily basis."

Their response is, "Oh, so you do advertising, social media, email…" They immediately drill right down to the tactical level, which, again, is only partially correct.

Though the tactics are key in driving the actions of a marketing plan, they are not the full scope of the power of marketing. We need to dive deeper and take a look at the root of marketing.

In its simplicity, marketing is "the act of encouraging, shifting or changing a behavior to drive purchasing consideration for a product or service."

There's a key word in my definition. Marketing is really about how we shape *behavior* to get individuals to perform in a certain way.

It comes down to the psychology of how individuals actually buy, and why they buy. It's how your product or service helps them solve a problem, a challenge, or simply satisfy a need or want.

In its simplicity, marketing is "the act of encouraging, shifting, or changing a behavior to drive purchasing consideration for a product or service.

Preface

MARKETING ENCOMPASSES A STRATEGIC PROCESS

It's a process where you first understand who you are, what you stand for, what is your promise, and how are you going to deliver on that promise. These four components are the foundation for your brand—your identity in the marketplace. Understanding your brand is the very foundation of your marketing efforts.

With a better understanding of your brand, you must then focus on your buyers. Who are your customers? What do they need from your company? And, where are your customers, so you can determine the best means to communicate with them?

That's really how you can employ the force of marketing—understanding you, understanding your company, understanding your customer, and the environment around that customer.

MARKETING IS SUCCESSFUL

It's interesting; a number of companies come to me and say, "I tried marketing and it didn't work." Well, for marketing to be effective, along with a strategic process, it needs to be planned and executed well, and be *continually* refined over a period of time.

Preface

Marketing will never be a one-hit wonder; it's a continual activity that is honed and scaled. I refer to it as "strategize, plan, execute, analyze, rinse, and repeat."

Preface

Preface

Marketing is Mighty

It has the influence to increase your brand authority, credibility, client base, revenue, and scale of your company.

In the following pages of this book, I will walk **you** through my proven process that I have implemented countless times to help my clients get clarity, focus, and phenomenal results. Every chart and worksheet is included again at the end of the book for your own use.

Ready to harness the power of marketing?

Let's get started!

Chapter One

YOUR BRAND: KNOWING AND EXPRESSING YOUR WHY AND VALUE

UNDERSTANDING WHO YOU ARE, who your company is, and the value you bring to your customers is the foundation for your brand and purpose behind your marketing. It's how you tell your story, express your promise, and provide a unique resolution to your customers' challenges, needs, and wants.

It's your brand identity, your expressive voice within your company and throughout your marketplace and sphere of influence. And, most importantly, it must be defined *before* you venture into any marketing planning or activities. If you don't know who you are or where you are going, how do you know how to get there? More importantly, how can your customers know who you are if you don't?

> I tell my clients, if you don't know who you are or where you are going, how do you know how to get there? More importantly, how can your customers know who you are if you don't?

Before we take the step into the realm of how to create your brand identity, let's debunk some common myths and mislabeling of your "brand."

Your brand is not your logo

Yes, your logo is the symbol of your brand, but it is not the only piece. When consumers see your logo, they should get a sense of your company's voice, if not your entire mission. Before designing your logo, you should already have a full working knowledge of what your brand is – who you are, what you stand for, and why you are different. Otherwise, your logo will not elicit the emotional connection and understanding you want your brand to project.

YOUR BRAND IS NOT YOUR TAGLINE

A great tagline can say so much about your brand. That's why many make the mistake of thinking the tagline *is* the brand. But a tagline changes over time based upon differing connection points with your customers, while your brand vision remains the same. You can't even write the catchy words until you know your brand inside and out.

YOUR BRAND IS NOT YOUR PRODUCT OR SERVICE BENEFITS

Of course, you should tout the benefits and features of your product or service. These are factors that add value to your brand. They are not, however, the brand itself. Your brand is not one tangible thing; it's aspirational, inspirational, and your intrinsic value.

Your Brand Identity

So, what is your brand identity, and how is it developed? A number of methodologies have been developed over the years that provide theoretical philosophies and analytic models, but it doesn't have to be complicated. It needs to be clear, concise, simple, and fun.

When working with my clients, I guide them through a multi-step process that I have successfully employed for many years. It takes into account a person and/or company's internal and external environments and a number of key indicators that shape current perceptions, future ambitions and benefits.

Let's start with the internal and external environments, as both will have a role in shaping your brand. Internally is defined as understanding the current brand beliefs and perceptions of company stakeholders, customers, partners, and affiliates.

If it's your personal brand, then you must look at individuals in your influential chain. Externally, analyze your competition.

- How do they look?
- What does your audience say about them?
  How are they positioning themselves?
- What is their product offering?

You also need to look at the marketplace to access any trends, news, challenges, and the availability of secondary research.

Your Marketing Road Map

YOU NEED TO DO YOUR HOMEWORK

It's critical to have an understanding of everything that could and will impact your brand position. Building your brand identity is not shaped only by internal sources; it takes external knowledge to define your difference.

Your brand must stand out in the marketplace. If it doesn't, then your company is another "me too," giving your customers no reason to buy from you instead of a competitor.

Once you have gathered this information, it's always a good idea to compile a SWOT analysis: Strength, Weakness, Opportunities, and Threats. This will provide a clearer picture of your brand opportunities and potential negatives, as well as help shape your marketing plan.

Brand Attributes

Now that we have all the facts and research taken care of, how do we create the actual mechanics of your brand identity?

A strong brand identity is based upon a number of

elements, with the first element determining your brand attributes.

What are brand attributes? They are three to five things that your company stands for or aspires to.

To determine your attributes, review the information you obtained during your fact-finding discussions with internal stakeholders, customers, partners and affiliates. Look to their comments around current perceptions, strengths, and beliefs.

Your Marketing Road Map

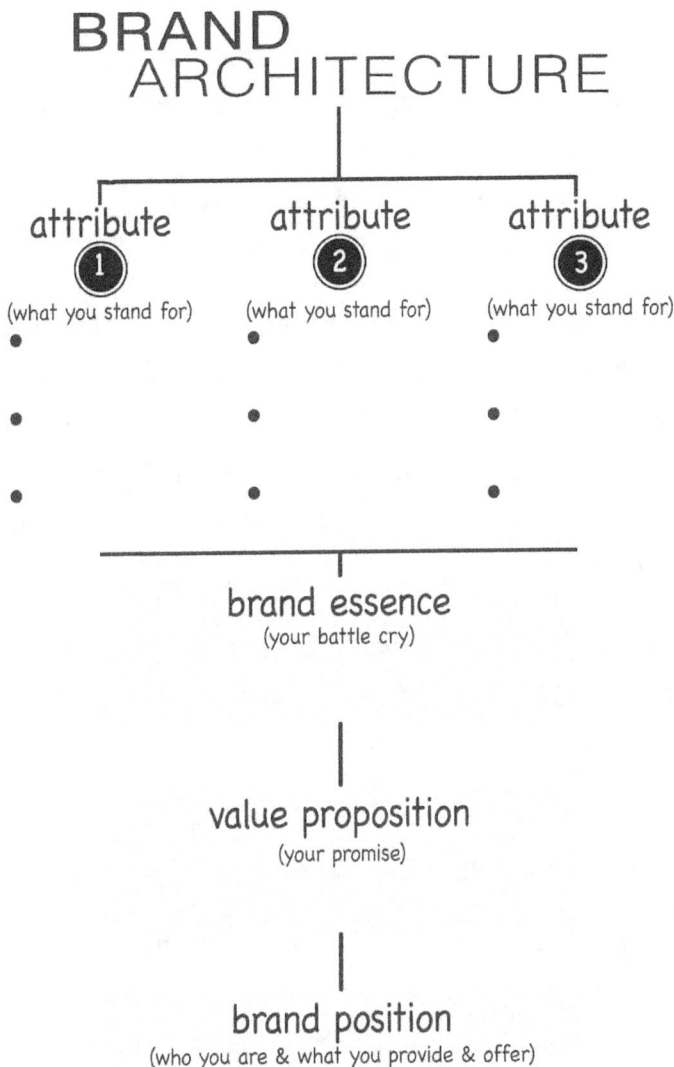

For example, one of my clients, a major food and beverage company, was looking to expand their sales channels beyond contract manufacturing to developing their own branded product lines. Meaning, we needed to not only build the company brand, but also the product brand extension as well.

We employed our external/internal research and analysis as stated above, and developed three key attributes. The first attribute was *heritage and tradition* to express the strong influence a thirty-year-old family-owned business had both internally and externally.

The second attribute was *premium nutritional products*, which encompassed the company's passion to provide healthy products.

The third was *humanitarian* for their unwavering dedication to community outreach and philanthropy.

Another client example is a company that provides medical products and services to hospitals and medical facilities. What makes this example particularly interesting is that we needed to build a brand based on the merger of three companies by taking into account the perceptions of three distinct entities and bringing them together as one.

Again, we utilized our research and analysis process, and established three distinct attributes: The first, expertise, to showcase their longevity and in-depth knowledge based on the criticality of this particular attribute in healthcare; second, service, to express both the staff's exceptional ability as well as their competitive difference; and third, passion, to represent their people-focused culture and always-deliver attitude.

Brand Essence and Promise

The next brand identity element is discovering your brand essence—your battle cry. What gets you excited? What is your absolute passion? For my food and beverage client, is was "live well' to depict their passion for providing health-based products. For the medical products and service client, their essence was "gratification guaranteed" to demonstrate both their internal culture and dedication to serving their clients.

We now move on to developing the most important part of your brand identity, and that is your value proposition—your promise. This communicates what your brand is going to deliver to your customers and one of the distinguishing reasons for connecting with your brand.

Let's go back to the two company examples. For the food and beverage company, their promise is to "provide healthy and naturally good-for-you products that taste great." You will notice that we brought in the emotional appeal of their essence, "live well," and their healthy products attribute. Also, as we know, there is a preconceived notion that healthy products don't taste good, so we wanted to make sure we addressed this to eliminate that correlation.

For the medical products and service company, their promise, which is also their competitive distinction, is to "provide seamless healthcare product purchases through delivery installation and support," which brings in the appeal of their essence and service attribute.

Once you have developed your attributes, your essence, and your value, you then combine those to create your brand positioning statement. This is a statement that expresses your why—why you want to soothe your customers' pain points and solve their problems. What drives you to provide the best products and services for your buyers?

Your Brand Story

As the brand identity is the structure of your brand and outlines your brand's key components, you also need to express the passion behind the brand and the reason why you do what you do: Your Brand Story. This is the emotional appeal of your brand.

> Statistics state that 100% of individuals, whether they are making a purchase for business or personal needs, make decisions based on emotion. Period.

Why is this important? For one, statistics state that one hundred percent of individuals, whether they are making a purchase for business or personal needs, make decisions based on emotion. Period. Two, we are living in a hyper-social world, built on emotion-based triggers—community building, sharing, and immediate gratification.

You need to build your brand on a deeper level to create meaningful relationships. Individuals buy from companies they know, like, and trust. You need to construct a connection so you have the opportunity to nurture a relationship and gain trust, so when your customers are ready to buy, they buy from your brand.

To help craft a brand story, I always tell my clients to remember *why* the company was created in the first place. Was it triggered by a life event, a certain circumstance or need that had to be fulfilled? Was it a passion, a life's mission that needed to be realized?

For me, my brand story was created by a passion and need. I have always had a passion for marketing and helping my clients and individuals to succeed; this gives me joy and a feeling of great satisfaction.

But for many years my spirit, self, and passion was being compromised by toeing the line for others' companies, where company came first, and self and family a distant second. Since I had senior-level positions, I worked long hours, which took time away from my personal experiences. I got tired of seeing pictures of my family, minus mommy. I got tired of being tired and stressed, which had a direct effect on my family and me.

So, one day I decided that I wanted to keep doing what I loved, work with great clients, and be there for my family when they needed me, not when it was convenient for a business. And I never looked back. Today, I have a successful company and am enjoying every entrepreneurial minute, every day, all day. Of course, I continue to work long hours, but those hours are now on my terms.

With my *why* firmly in place, my brand story goes on to express my promise, position, and what I deliver.

As you can see, my story provides meaningful, authentic insight into my brand, and clearly defines my why and purpose. Any established business owner, which happens to be one my business targets, would either directly relate with my story, or my story would spur their thoughts about their why. Either way, I have reached them on a deeper emotional level, which subconsciously starts building rapport, relationship, and trust.

Take this opportunity to think about your why, your purpose, and combine this with brand identity to shape your perfect story.

Building an emotional connection is an important part of any brand.

Chapter Two

YOUR CUSTOMER: UNDERSTANDING THE WHOLE PERSONA

IN CHAPTER ONE, we talked a little bit about understanding the customer and their challenges and pain points, and how your brand needs to be positioned to provide a unique solution.

Yes, solving a problem is key to gaining customer interest, but it is not the only thing that drives deep-rooted relationships with your customers.

You need to go beyond the statistical data of demographics and lifestyle models, and really look at more emotional, life stage and functional components that drive decisions.

You need to understand your customer
from a 360° perspective.

You need to understand your customer from a 360° perspective. You need to create, as we refer to them in marketing, your customer personas. This means you must define your ideal buyer's characteristics from both a business and personal standpoint, including their influential chain.

An influential chain are those individuals or circumstances that affect the buying behaviors of others. The people who affect a buyer's behavior might be your customer's family, colleagues, or friends.

An influential life stage or occurrence, such as an engagement, divorce, child heading to college or just starting kindergarten could qualify as part of the influential chain. Whatever the conditions, your customer's life experiences have a direct correlation on their buying behavior.

Your Marketing Road Map

PERSONA
CREATION

#1 demographics
-
-
-

#2 background
-
-
-

#3 interest
-
-
-

#4 goals
-
-
-

#5 pain points & challenges
-
-
-

#6 shopping & communication preference
-
-
-

To demonstrate, let's look at one of your fictional customers, Sally Smith. We know that she is the Operations Director at ABC Company, with two hundred employees and annual revenues of $100 million. We also know that she is responsible for making the buying decisions for enterprise-wide software, one of your product offerings.

We assume that she is between forty-five to fifty-five years old, because reaching a director-level position requires time and experience to achieve. We can also assume that, due to the nature of a director's job, time, budget and lack of internal resources affects her software purchases.

This is great information, because you know she is responsible for making decisions on your product offering, and that your products can soothe some of her pain points. But you really only scratched the surface in understanding Sally as a whole person.

Yes, the information you have will help with getting some sales, but what about Sally's long-term value to your company? Do you have enough information to sustain her relationship over time? The answer is most likely no.

Innate Persona Development

Let's dig deeper and expand on Sally's personal background and role in the company.

- Is she married, single, divorced?
- Does she have children, and if so how many, what are their names and ages?
- What's her education level?
- What are her hobbies?
- What does she like to do in her spare time?
- What does she value most—job security, family, recognition for success, church?
- From a business perspective, what are her duties?
- What is her performance measured by?
- Does she have staff?
- How much staff does she have?

Knowing her personal and work responsibilities, demands, and values enables you to have a deeper understanding of her current situation, so you can tailor your conversations and interactions to best build trust and value.

You also need an expanded view into her goals and

challenges, even though they may not have a direct correlation with her decision to buy and interact with your company. These factors may influence her perceptions, thoughts, and purchasing decisions.

Lastly, and extremely important, you need to understand her shopping and communication preferences. Does she prefer to receive communication through email, phone, or text? Does she use the internet to search for products and services? What about industry or trade publications? Does she attend trade shows? What about social networking sites like LinkedIn?

Having this information will help shape your connections and determine the tactics to use in your marketing plan.

PERSONA WORKSHEET

Archetypes

An additional reference point to help you understand the emotional and behavioral side of persona development is to look over the twelve common archetypes defined by famed psychologist Carl Jung, who used the concept in his theory of the human psyche.

He believed that certain archetypes resided within the collective unconscious of individuals, with each type having a set of values, meanings, and personality traits. And, that most, if not all, people had several archetypes at play in their personality structure, with one tending to dominate the personality.

Each of these archetypes has its own strategy, fear, desire, weakness, and goal. Identifying the archetypes residing in each of your buyers will help you better understand what motivates and drives them. These archetypes, as explained by Jung, are outlined as follows:

- The Innocent
- The Orphan
- The Hero
- The Caregiver

- The Explorer
- The Rebel
- The Lover
- The Creator
- The Jester
- The Sage
- The Magician
- The Ruler

Even the names of these archetypes give you some insight into the buyers whose personality might encompass them. A deeper dig into each will tell you so much more about the psychology of your customers. In the end, it is all about understanding your customer's behavior and influences, so they initially buy and continually buy your products and services. It's understanding their buying journey, and how to communicate with them each step of the way.

The Buyer's Journey

Think of the buyer's journey as a bridge that connects a prospect to your brand, and split that bridge into three parts:

- The Awareness Stage

- The Consideration Stage
- The Decision Stage

To guide the buyer across, you have to tailor your content and communication to each stage.

The Awareness Stage

During this first stage, the buyers, your potential customers, experience some type of problem and begin the search for a solution. They will educate themselves and discover possible avenues for resolution.

At this stage, they more than likely do not want to talk to your sales person and probably couldn't care less about your brand. The goal at this stage is to educate them by providing quality, helpful materials like expert guides, tip sheets, check lists, and more.

These introduce the buyers to your brand and, more importantly, show that you understand their problem and know exactly how to help.

The Consideration Stage

The buyer is able to define their problem and knows exactly what solution or opportunity they need. As they were aware of your brand in the awareness stage, they are now more willing to hear about what you can do for them.

This is not the time for a hard sell; it is time to educate them on your merits, successes, and possibly how you solved a similar problem for another customer.

You can do this through case studies, free samples, and testimonials. In this stage, you will start to construct the relationship and build trust.

Decision Making Stage

In the final phase in the buyer's journey, they are now ready to buy and need to know why your solution is the best. Show them through free trials, demonstrations, and special offers. You have them on the hook, so reel them in.

Too many companies end the cycle there, with little to no focus on how to make the customer return for future purchases. Studies have shown that acquiring a customer costs more than keeping one, so why wouldn't you focus on driving customers right back to the consideration stage?

Never miss a chance to follow up with your buyers after the purchase is complete. Start with a sincere thank you, and then continue to provide excellent information about the products and services you sell.

Use the information you gathered about your customer during their search to share relevant, helpful information that keeps them coming back for more.

Do you know your whole customer? If not, it's time to find out. Your business growth depends on it.

When you nab that customer, then you need to encourage them to be your cheerleader.

Chapter Three

YOUR COMMUNICATION: EXPRESSING THE BENEFIT IN THE MESSAGE

YOU NOW HAVE your distinct brand and a much better understanding of your customers. Let's take all that info and make it sing.

Shout it from the rooftops. Let all your customers, and potential customers know how you are going to catapult them and their businesses to greatness.

Your success relies on properly constructing the message that expresses both your brand and value, while speaking directly to your customer persona groups, solving their pain and challenges, and satisfying their need. It's about developing a message hierarchy that stays true to your brand, your one voice, while taking into account the specific group requirements.

Your success relies on properly constructing the message that expresses both your brand and value, while speaking directly to your customer persona groups, solving their pain and challenges, and satisfying their need.

Messaging Components

So, how do you get started?

You begin by looking at the key messaging components of your brand. These are the overarching components of what makes up your brand and product or service. They are constructed by referencing your brand identity components and developing key points that quantify those components.

For example, let's go back to my food and beverage client. Their product brand messaging components were as follows: corporate brand, product category, taste great, health and nutritional products, and good for the entire family. For the medical products company, the components included experience, service, and product depth.

Once you have your messaging components, you then extend those components to your target groups.

When I work with my clients, I have them visualize it as an umbrella. The tiptop of the umbrella is your brand: who you are, and what you stand for.

The spokes of the umbrella are your customer personas, and the raindrops running down each section are messages that are specific to their circumstances and how your brand satisfies their needs.

When you apply an understanding that larger organizations have other layers, divisions, and products per division, the concept remains the same.

Extend your brand story and value through your hierarchy, while providing your customer solutions and value along the way.

MESSAGING
WORKSHEET

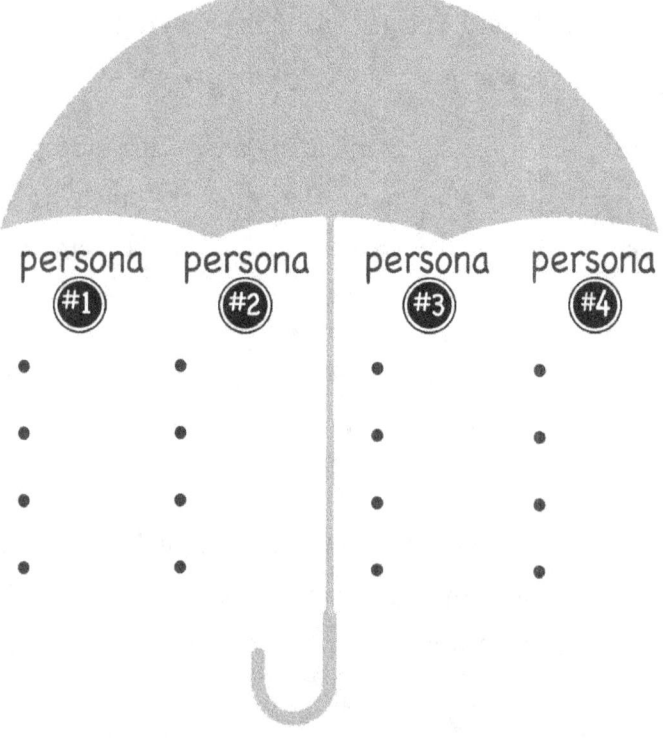

To illustrate how this works, I want to highlight another one of my clients where we had to not only build their brand, but also take complex subject matter and properly message it to very distinct audiences.

The client is a financial services company that combines consultation with senior-level staffing through search- and partner-based programs. They also have a proprietary technology that enables this unique combination to be readily available to its clientele.

One attribute we created was innovation based on their technology, and another was passion for developing cutting-edge, first-to-market programs.

With one such program, we had to communicate its value to organizations that would hire my client to utilize the program, and also to recruit qualified personnel to be a participant in the program.

For the organizations, the message was "With the integration of our highly talented base and search technology, [client's] resources and experience are highly sought after in the industry."

The program message to participants was "[Client] is the only firm that has a dedicated program focused solely on helping you continue and further advance your career through on-going training/mentoring and..."

As you can see, we promoted the same program, but the messaging benefits expressed were based on the explicit necessities of the target personas.

The Magic of Language

Proper messaging is about knowing your brand and your target, yes, but it is also about using proper language and words. As a student of language with love for the written word, I understand first hand that strategically using the right words can invoke certain emotions and actions.

For instance, if you want someone to take action, you must use action words like stop, go, clap, chew. If we want to compel them to do something, we need to have action words with directional narrative, such as:

- Don't wait; get your copy today.
- Hurry while supplies last.
- Register now, early bird special ends today.

Also, one word can change the context or meaning of your message. For example, take a look at the two following sentences. They focus on the same subject matter, but use differing language.

I will take care of that today.

I should take care of that today.

By changing one word, will to should, the meaning behind the sentence goes from an affirmed action to a questionable action.

Proper messaging is about knowing your brand and your target, yes, but it is also about using proper language and words... Strategically using the right words can invoke certain emotions and actions.

Ready to create your message? Don't fret; you don't have to be a professional writer. If you understand your brand, personas, and the benefit your company provides, it's just a matter of expressing this value through relevant, benefit-oriented language. And remember, it's always all about the customer.

Relevant content is imperative.

Chapter Four

YOUR LOOK: CREATING THE VISUAL SIDE OF YOUR BRAND

AS I MENTIONED in earlier chapters, building a brand is not just about the function; it is also about building the emotion and affinity for your brand.

Yes, messaging is extremely important, but it is also much more impactful when it is concurrently represented in visual form. How you visually represent your brand is as significant as how you verbally—both spoken and written—express your brand.

Think about how your mind works. When you hear something, your brain starts to decipher the messages. When you couple that with a visual of that message, the stimulation takes on much more meaning and provides a more powerful sensory experience.

> How you visually represent your brand is as significant as how you verbally express your brand.

Consider the explosive growth of video. According to Online Publishers Association, eighty percent of users can recall a video ad they have seen in the last thirty days. And, as reported by ComScore, the average user spends over sixteen minutes watching video ads each month—staggering engagement and interaction numbers for sure.

Let's take a look at the other end of the spectrum: traditional print advertising. Yes, individuals do still subscribe to magazines. Print publications continue to be a great way to reach specific target groups, if that is the channel those particular groups use to gather information on making buying decisions.

This is particularly true in the business-to-business marketing arena, where niche industry trade publications are still revered as great sources of information.

Why?

A number of individuals are also very tactile and want physical stimulation along with visual perception.

In this case, we need to go back to Advertising 101, where it was imperative that the message in your headline worked directly with the visual component of the ad to tell your story. The copy then provided context to support the story.

Today, this practice is still influential in delivering your message and difference, with added direct response components to get individuals to not only read, but also act on the information.

Whichever channel or creative platform you use as part of your marketing plan, the visual component clearly holds a lot of weight in building your brand. So, how do we make sure our visuals are on point?

Colors Emotion

Color is all around us. It shapes our thoughts, perceptions, moods, and reactions. It subconsciously affects our behaviors, actions, and how we feel—good or bad.

Think about it.

Why do so many healthcare related products and institutions use the color blue? Because blue depicts trustworthiness, dignity, and serenity.

Financial institutions use green because it is the color of money. Green also projects environmental, harmony, and nature, and as such, is heavily used to support sustainability causes, companies, and initiatives.

Fast food restaurants use the color red because it grabs attention and induces hunger.

And, traffic light colors weren't haphazardly chosen; they were chosen for the subliminal reactions. Red means danger; the reaction is stop. Yellow means caution; the reaction is slow down. Green means renewal; the reaction is go.

COLOR MEANINGS

black
authority
boldness
classic
conservative
death
distinctive
exclusive
formality
misery
mystery
secrecy
seriousness
tradition

blue
authority
calm
confidence
dignity
established
loyalty
power
serenity
success
secure
tranquility
trustworthy

brown
calmness
depth
earth
natural
roughness
richness
simplicity
serious
subtle
utility
woodsy

green
crisp
environmental
freshness
harmony
health
healing
inexperience
money
nature
renewal
tranquility

grey
authority
corporate mentality
dullness
humility
mooduy
practicality
respect
somberness
stability

orange
adventurous
affordable
confident
creativity
enthusiasm
fun
jovial
lighthearted
high-spirited
youthful

COLOR MEANINGS

appreciation
delicate
femininity
floral
gentle
girly
gratitude
innocence
romantic
softness
tranquility

beauty
ceremony
expensive
fanasy
inspiration
justice
magic
mystey
nobility
regal
royalty
sophistication
spirituality
wonder

action
adventure
agression
blood
danger
drive
enegy
excitement
love
passion
power
romance
strength
vigor

communication
commitment
credibility
reliability
spiritual
  advancement
trustworthiness

caution
cheerfulness
cowardice
curiosity
happiness
joy
playfulness
positivity
sunshine
warmth
wisdom

white
cleanliness
innnocence
peace
purity
refined
sterile
simplocity
surrender
truthfulness

Fonts Speak

Like color, typography is everywhere. It also shapes our subconscious feelings and reactions, and builds associated perceptions.

Have you ever received an email typed in capitalized, bold font? What was your reaction? Perhaps it was, "Why are they shouting at me?" Did you want to continue reading it? You probably did not.

How about a tech company using a script font? Would you feel that they were innovative and analytical, or more creative? You'd likely assume the latter.

When selecting fonts, take into account the medium in which your message is displayed. You wouldn't want to use a stylistic font on a website due to readability issues, or a narrow font on a billboard. Look at the same message below, displayed in different fonts. What are these fonts saying to you?

Marketing Is Powerful

Marketing Is Powerful

Marketing Is Powerful

Marketing Is Powerful

LIZ PAPAGNI

TRENDING FONTS

Avenir "The quick brown fox jumps over the lazy dog."

Baskerville "The quick brown fox jumps over the lazy dog."

Century Schoolbook "The quick brown fox jumps over the lazy dog."

Courier "The quick brown fox jumps over the lazy dog."

Franklin Gothic "The quick brown fox jumps over the lazy dog."

Futura "The quick brown fox jumps over the lazy dog."

Garamond "The quick brown fox jumps over the lazy dog."

Georgia "The quick brown fox jumps over the lazy dog."

Gill Sans "The quick brown fox jumps over the lazy dog."

Gotham "The quick brown fox jumps over the lazy dog."

Helvetica Neue "The quick brown fox jumps over the lazy dog."

Hoefler Text "The quick brown fox jumps over the lazy dog."

Minion "The quick brown fox jumps over the lazy dog."

Shapes Mood

Regardless if a shape is flat, 2D or 3D, they influence our subconscious. Like colors and fonts, shapes help mold our emotions, feelings, and behavior.

To demonstrate their possible effects, we chose basic root shapes of circular, square, rectangles, and triangles, along with lines, curves, and angles.

LIZ PAPAGNI

SHAPE MEANINGS

circular

tenderness
love
friendship
care
support
protection
affection
compassion

squares rectangles triangles

stability
strength
power
balance
reliability

vertical shapes or lines

strength
masculinity
power
aggression
courage
brutality
domination
menacing

horizontal lines

tranquility
feminine
calm
rest
weak
peaceful
composed
silent
still
non-menacing

soft curves

rhythm
movement
happiness
pleasure
generosity
femininity

sharp angles

energy
lively
young
explosive
violent
anger
rapidity
dynamic
movement

So what does this all mean for your brand? The colors, fonts, and creative elements you use have a direct effect on how your target groups will visually perceive your brand. What is the main visual *symbol* of your brand? Your company logo.

Your look all starts with a well-crafted, purposeful logo. A logo that *directly* projects the brand identity and messaging we defined and outlined in Chapters 1 and 2, and is relevant and meaningful to your target personas as discussed in Chapter 3.

Your logo sets the foundation for your fonts, creative elements, and color palette, which will then all be used to form the creation of your collateral, ads, website, and more.

With such importance to your brand identity, the design of your logo should be well thought out and executed. As with building your brand identity, messaging, and target personas, this too is an investment area.

Hire a professional—not just a creative genius, but one that understands the strategic and emotional meaning behind the brand. Creative is only as good as the detailed grasp of the foundational story behind the brand. Fonts, colors, shapes, etc. are chosen by the designer solely based on the story.

The temptation to use discounted design services from amateurs or even graphic design interns may be too great to ignore.

Be cautious.

Regardless of how great a graphic designer's previous work may look, it's important to gauge your chosen professional's understanding of your brand before you engage them for work.

Without that solid grasp on your brand story, your target audience, and your brand aesthetics, you could receive a logo that has zero impact on or connection with your brand. I tell my clients, garbage in, garbage out. Period.

As you go through the logo design process, there are some universal design guidelines to consider.

Simplicity

Logos don't have to be intricate and complicated to get your message across. Keep it simple, clean, and concise, as long as it projects your brand affinity.

Think Apple, Nike, and McDonalds. There is something to be said about the old adage "less is more."

Memorable

As an extension of simplicity, you also want your logo to be memorable. Good logos feature something diverse, unusual and/or unexpected without overwhelming, which makes them easy to remember due to their uniqueness. Look at Target and Starbucks.

Versatile

Your logo should be easily adaptable for various marketing mediums, applications, and usage. When I present logos to my client, I always present them in color, reversed-out white and black, with both horizontal and vertical versions. This enables them to see how effective the logo would be given different circumstances and applications.

The visual component of your brand is a vital part of expressing your story and difference.

Embrace it. Create it. And reap the benefits.

Chapter Five

YOUR MARKETING PLAN: MAKING SENSE OF THE PARTS AND PIECES...INCLUDING DIGITAL

IN CHAPTERS 1 THROUGH 4, we built the necessary foundational brand and messaging components, including an in-depth understanding of the market and competitive landscape and your customers, particularly their communication preferences.

This information provides clarity on the Overview, Situation Analysis, Target Audience, and Messaging Sections of your marketing plan, including some directional information on channel selection.

The two core components of the plan, Objectives and Strategies, shape the main purpose and outcomes, and drive the plan execution.

LIZ PAPAGNI

MARKETING PLAN
FRAMEWORK

- **overview** (summary of plan, reasoning & purpose)

- **situation analysis**
  (state of market/competition your brand difference/value)

- **target audience** (persona descritpions)

- **goals** (what you are trying to accomplish)

- **strategies** (how you are to meet your goals)

- **execution** (channel selections, budget allocations, calendar flow)

- **measurement/analysis** (kpi's and plan assessment)

Plan Goals

Goals are simply what you want to achieve with your marketing plan. What is the end result of your efforts?

Is it to build awareness? Build engagement and brand interaction? Increase your potential customer base? Create thought leadership?

In most cases, you will have more than one goal.

The key is to choose those that are most important, which will keep your plan more focused and the goals attainable.

If you try to accomplish too much, your efforts will become disjointed and scattered, producing lackluster results. Think clarity, focus, and purpose.

Plan Strategies

Your strategy is an outline of how you will achieve your objectives—the overarching guidance to the execution portion of the plan.

For instance, if one goal were to increase your potential client base, then you would employ a lead generation strategy.

Within this lead generation strategy, you would

outline a content strategy (messaging), offer strategy (entice prospects to give contact information), call-to-action strategy (specific directive to influence customer behavior), and a channel strategy (the mediums where your messages will reside, i.e. social media, email, print).

Plan Execution

The channels you choose are a strategic combination of your target persona preferences, your goals, and your strategies. There is a key word in this sentence: strategic.

As I alluded to in the Preface, too many times companies go right to the tactics without building the right foundation and wonder why their marketing falls short.

The most effective, results-driven, and executable plans come from the time and effort that is put into developing the right base. This is imperative.

STRATEGIC PLAN EXECUTION

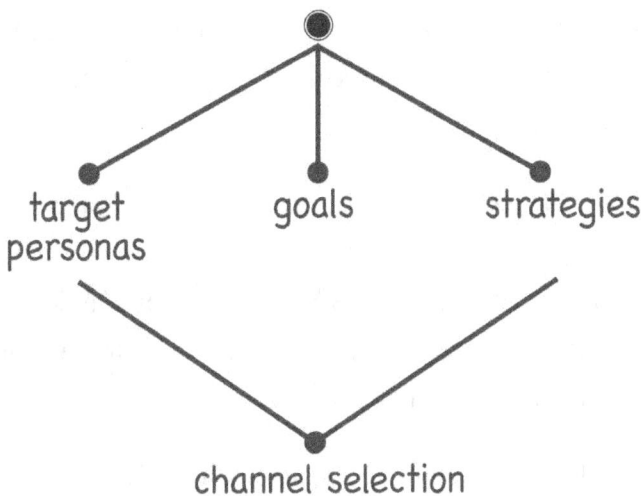

Let's look at your fictional customer Sally from Chapter 2. You conducted some additional research and found that she uses online search and trade publications to gather product information and prefers email communications. She is married with two teenage daughters, and one of her performance measures at work is reducing costs.

You also previously discovered that some of her pain points included lack of time, resources, and budget constraints. And one of your overall goals this year is to increase loyalty and sales with key accounts, with Sally being one of those accounts. So, how do you interpret that data to devise a channel strategy?

First, we know that Sally uses online and trade print publications to gather information and prefers email communications; these will be your communication channels. The question is how do you use these channels to meet your goals? Think strategically.

Email as a medium is not generally effective as an initial touch with prospects; it is more effective as a follow-up communication once the prospect has knowledge of you and/or your company. But Sally is already a customer and would more than likely open your email.

So, you use email to satisfy your loyalty goal and keep your company top-of-mind, and to help solidify your position as the vendor of choice when she is ready to buy.

Integrate online SEO (Search Engine Optimization) and Google AdWords so your company and product solutions appear in the search results when Sally does online product research.

Deploy a trade publication strategy that consists of public relations (unpaid media) and print advertising (paid media). Once again, Sally will see your company and products.

What does this accomplish? Sally continually receives your key messaging and reasons to choose your company, which dramatically increases her recall, affinity, and purchase consideration.

Now you need to get Sally to act. How? You provide her content and offers that lessen her pain points of lack of time, resources, and budget.

Through email, online ads, or in print, provide white papers or articles on tips, tutorials, or tricks to maximize her time and resources. For offers, provide free or discounted installation, training assistance, or after-purchase support.

And make sure your overall content uses language that evokes simplicity, ease of use, quickness, cost-effectiveness, and overall value.

Most importantly, think integration and synergy. You

want all your executions to work together to achieve optimal impact, effectiveness, and efficiency.

Plan Measurement & Analysis

You built a strong brand foundation. You know your customers inside and out. You developed a plan based on your customer, your goals, and your strategies. Awesome.

Now you need to outline how you are going to measure the effectiveness of your plan. Is it number of leads, email opens, social media fans? Whatever it is, be sure to include this as part of the overall plan. These metrics will enable you to analyze the effectiveness of each tactic and make adjustments to continue to maximize your plans effectiveness. As I mentioned before, I call this "strategize, plan, execute, analyze, rinse and repeat."

The Digital Explosion

SEO, PPC, blogs, content aggregators, Facebook, Pinterest, Instagram, Snapchat, TikTok, LinkedIn, Twitter, hashtags…

Oh, my! Is your head spinning yet? Well, you aren't alone.

> Digital is a force and needs to be part of your marketing strategy.

The scope of digital marketing changes daily, and so do the offerings and utilization. Digital is a force and needs to be part of your marketing strategy. You definitely need to be in the game, but it doesn't have to be difficult.

Think of it this way: it's purely another communication strategy that you have in your arsenal to get your brand and message in front of customers and prospects.

Like any marketing resource, you only choose those tactics that meet your strategy, objectives, and target personas. And, contrary to some elitists' beliefs, it doesn't replace traditional marketing; digital integrates with traditional marketing to provide a more robust plan of action.

So, take a deep breath. Exhale. It's all good.

We'll take things one at time, starting with your website.

Your Website

We can't really talk about digital marketing without starting with the most important piece: your website.

When building your website, you'll need to take all of the previous aspects of marketing we've discussed—your brand, your customer, your communication, and your look—and combine them with your digital strategy.

Regardless of how large or small your business may be, your customers expect to see your website when they search for you online. Making sure your website is optimized for mobile devices is also crucial.

When developed correctly, your website becomes one of your most powerful marketing tools.

Search Engine Optimization

In the simplest of terms, search engine optimization, or SEO, is all about getting found online. The key to a good SEO strategy is *quality* traffic, and not just quantity—and all from unpaid sources, rather than direct or paid traffic.

Good SEO practices involve more than just keywords, though relevant search phrases are the cornerstone of a good SEO strategy.

Don't just focus on the shorter phrases, either, as you'll battle your competitors daily for the results.

Focus instead on some long-tail search phrases that will reach buyers who are closer to making a purchasing decision than those who are just starting their search with simple keywords.

For additional boosts to your SEO, be sure to use meta data wherever you can, including titles and meta descriptions on images and video.

Every page on your website should have a meta description, too, with attention to key phrases that appear on that page—as long as those phrases are also relevant to the services you want people to find through searches.

Finally, test the speed on your site often, especially if you use video and images a lot. Google gives preference to faster sites, and so do buyers.

Content Marketing

Your marketing content, blogs, social media posts, published articles, videos, and any other words you share—however you may share them—serve to educate your buyers so they know the exact benefits they receive from your brand.

Map out the content your buyers need, how you plan to deliver that information, and where your buyers are most likely to consume it.

Prepare content for every stage of the buyer's journey so you can reach them at any time, wherever they may be in the decision-making process, but give special attention to those who have just started their search for a solution.

Google wants to see good quality content with their web crawlers, and they tend to return results with fresh content over websites that don't update very often.

The more content you publish, such as landing pages and blogs, the more content you'll give Google to index for higher ranking on search engine result pages.

Pay-Per-Click

Pay-per-click, or PPC, is an internet advertising model that drives traffic to your website, most likely a landing page created specifically for the product or service you wish to highlight or draw attention to.

You can fight over keywords and search phrases to show up in organic searches as often as possible, but you can also give those results a boost by showing up very first in the promoted section of the results.

As you create your PPC campaigns, keep the buyer's journey in mind. Create landing pages that meet every single step of the journey so that your potential customers have a chance to connect with you the moment they're ready.

Remember, give these ads some time to work. You will see an immediate increase in traffic, but the numbers may not match your expectations.

If you get frustrated and slash your PPC budget or, worse, cancel altogether, you'll lose the momentum you paid to build.

Social Media

Social media, in its purest definition, builds communities of like individuals around a common cause, brand, or product.

Social media, in its purest definition, builds communities of like individuals around a common cause, brand, or product...
Its influential ability is huge.

There's so much more to social media marketing than exposure and fan groups, though. You want to see your efforts affect your bottom line, right? The only way to do that is to focus on social media marketing activities that will convince your visitors to convert to buyers.

SOCIAL MEDIA ADVERTISING

All platforms allow you to target specific buyer groups through various categories, from geolocation to income levels. Focus on buyers with specific interests that align with your products, even if they've never heard of your brand. You can even target users who are friends or followers of your loyal customers in order to expand your potential audience.

Just be aware that your advertising must serve several purposes at once. First, you want to attract interest, which means your posts must be informative, eye-catching, and, for best results, entertaining.

Then, you can focus on driving the results you need.

You don't want to annoy anyone who comes across your ads, so be sure your targeting choices are relevant.

Retargeting Ads

A click doesn't always equal a purchase. Once those buyers visit your website or click through your social media marketing ads, you must continue to keep your products and brand top of mind through retargeting advertising.

This means your ads will continue to populate the users' social media feeds so they don't forget you.

If you don't put enough budget behind your social advertising in order to reach potential buyers over and over through retargeting, you could end up leaving a lot of money on the table.

Purchasing Buttons

The key to increasing revenue through social media marketing is to eliminate any friction between "want" and "buy." Social platforms understand this, and that's why several have introduced purchase buttons for brands to use with in tandem with their advertising images.

If you add a purchase button to your social media posts, then you can increase the possibility of a purchase, as you give the buyer less time to get distracted between seeing your product and making the decision to buy it.

Converting Fans to Customers

Your social media followers like something about your company; that is why they're followers. They are your captive audience, similar to a warm lead, so why not get them out of social media and into the sale process?

How?

Entice them with exclusive content and offers that require the submission of their contact information in order to receive the information.

Once they are in your database, they are now part of your prospecting funnel.

Remember, though: they are still a social media follower, so make sure that in your prospecting communications, you continue to address them as part of your community.

Brand Communities

What better way to create brand advocates than to bring them all together and let them chat about your products?

You have the chance to solve problems the moment they arise, which keeps the buyers happy and also generates a lot of goodwill.

Brand communities provide chances for you to convince potential buyers to take the leap and make a purchase. These communities, where your loyal customers share stories about your products, are the perfect places for new followers to ask questions and get genuine answers from past buyers.

This gives you valuable social proof that you just can't pay for with influencers, because they come from a place of honesty and authenticity.

Influencers

While genuine customers within your brand communities are valuable, don't rely entirely on those users to convince potential buyers. An influencer program—specifically micro influencers with small but dedicated audiences—can do a world of good for your bottom line.

These influencers often have higher engagement rates than mega influencers like celebrities because their audiences trust them to make honest recommendations based on their experiences.

When you work with influencers that are carefully chosen to support and magnify your brand, you can see a big difference in your social media conversion rates. Just be sure to fully vet your influencers or, better yet, work with an agency that has long-standing relationships with powerful and trustworthy influencers.

Chat Options

When your social media followers have questions about a product, you should be available as soon as possible to answer them. The time it takes for you to receive, read, and respond to an email could be long enough that the potential buyer has already become distracted or moved on to a competitor.

By offering chat or messaging options on your social media platforms, you can eliminate that lag and answer your buyers' questions right away. Without the ability to monitor your social media 24/7, you might consider installing a chatbot to answer some of the most common questions to keep the purchases moving.

Several high-tech AI options are available, all with the ability to learn and ask detailed questions of your buyers in order to give the best possible answers.

Platform Selection

Let's stop the impulse. *You don't have to be on every social media channel.* You should only be on those social media channels that your target audience uses.

Period.

If your buyer personas aren't teens or young twenty-somethings, then Snapchat isn't a necessity. If your company doesn't sell to other businesses, then LinkedIn won't help you.

Participation in two or three channels is the optimum

strategy. Why? As I have expressed in other chapters, marketing needs clarity, focus, and purpose.

You can't be focused and purposeful if you are trying to manage the content and interaction of more than three channels. You want to be able to dive deep and build strong communities and relationships, not cast a wide net that only skims the surface.

Authenticity

Individuals do business with companies they like, know, and trust. We build that rapport by expressing our true positions, feelings, integrity, and likeness.

The pure nature of social media is rooted in community, so it is imperative that you show authenticity in each and every post, *and* continually listen to and engage with your followers. I see too many companies who build non-benefit-oriented content, automate it with one of the social media scheduling tools, and then step away.

That is a waste of time, effort and budget dollars. It also has a high potential to have a negative effect on the brand. As research suggests, one bad review spreads 10 times faster than any good review. Be your authentic brand and reap the rewards.

Developing a results-driven marketing plan isn't difficult. It simply needs the proper framework, flexibility, and scalability.

Go for it!

Your success is in the plan.

About the Author

Liz Papagni is a leading brand and marketing strategist and CEO of Marketing Initiative Worx, Inc. As a marketing expert, she has launched and propelled brands for a range of clients, from Fortune 500 companies to small emerging businesses, developing killer brand strategies and marketing plans that take her clients' businesses to the next level. Liz serves as a Fractional CMO for companies that need the marketing strategy, planning, and execution a full-time Chief Marketing Officer and marketing team brings, but at a fraction of the cost. She is also a speaker on the topics of marketing and branding, and provides regular educational articles, tips, and how-to's on her Marketing Insights blog at marketingiw.com.

One Last Thing...

Thank you for reading Your Marketing Road Map. It is my sincere desire to help businesses of all sizes grow through excellent marketing and branding.

If you enjoyed this book or found it useful, I'd be very grateful if you'd post a short review on Amazon. Your support really does make a difference. I read all the reviews personally. Your feedback will make my next book even better.

Appendix

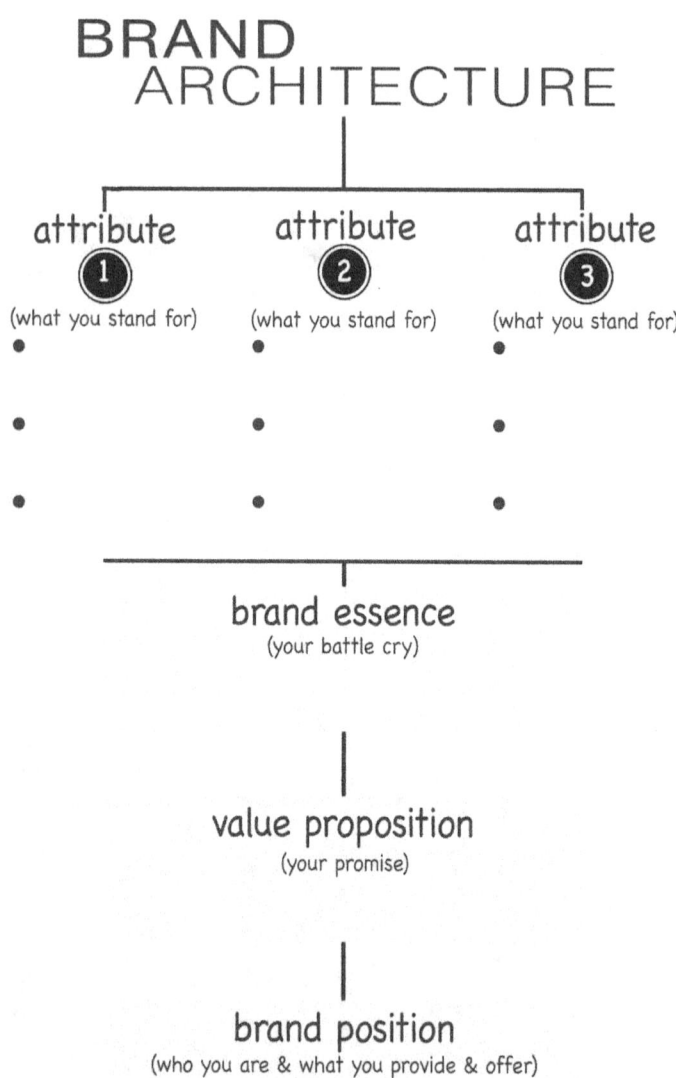

PERSONA CREATION

(#1) demographics
-
-
-

(#2) background
-
-
-

(#3) interest
-
-
-

(#4) goals
-
-
-

(#5) pain points & challenges
-
-
-

(#6) shopping & communication preference
-
-
-

Appendix

PERSONA
WORKSHEET

Appendix

MESSAGING
WORKSHEET

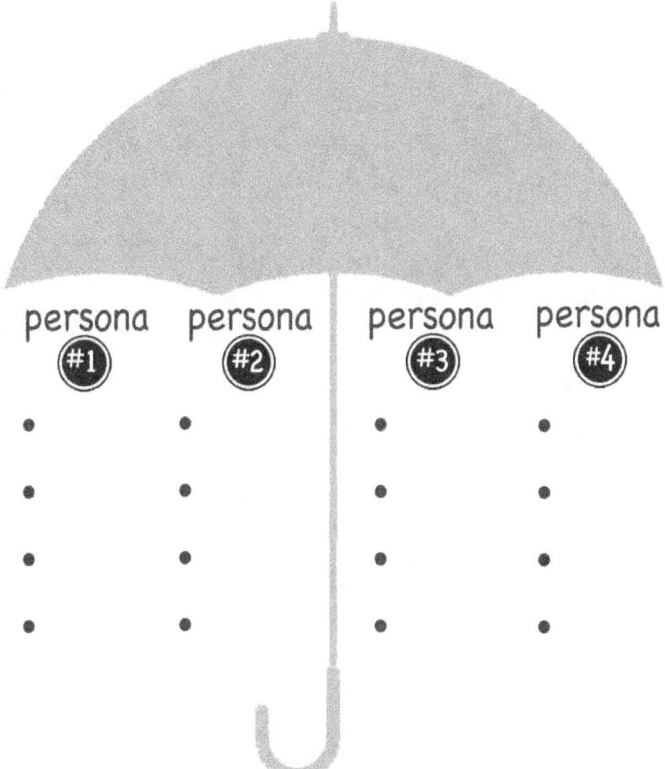

Appendix

MARKETING PLAN FRAMEWORK

- **overview** (summary of plan, reasoning & purpose)

- **situation analysis** (state of market/competition your brand difference/value)

- **target audience** (persona descritpions)

- **goals** (what you are trying to accomplish)

- **strategies** (how you are to meet your goals)

- **execution** (channel selections, budget allocations, calendar flow)

- **measurement/analysis** (kpi's and plan assessment)

Notes

Notes

Notes

www.ingramcontent.com/pod-product-compliance
Lightning Source LLC
Chambersburg PA
CBHW070433220526
45466CB00004B/1659